Creative Kittens
COLORING BOOK

Marjorie Sarnat

Dover Publications, Inc.
Mineola, New York

Kittens have a way of pulling at your heartstrings. This collection of fanciful designs will be no exception—especially after you've brought them to life with your own choice of colors! If you adore these four-legged companions, these 31 engaging images will be sure to appeal to your warm and fuzzy side. Intended for advanced colorists, these fantastical illustrations feature kittens adorned with typical markings such as stripes, spots, and patches, as well as imaginative ones—hearts, flowers, stars, paisley patterns, and much more. After coloring, remove the perforated pages from the book and display your beautiful artwork for everyone to see.

Bibliographical Note

Creative Kittens Coloring Book is a new work, first published
by Dover Publications, Inc., in 2017.

International Standard Book Number
ISBN-13: 978-0-486-81267-0
ISBN-10: 0-486-81267-7

Manufactured in the United States by LSC Communications
81267701   2017
www.doverpublications.com